T0110916

CONSCIOUS REFLECTION
Cultivating Self-Awareness in the Age of AI

IMPORTANCE OF SELF-AWARENESS IN THE AGE OF AI

Maria Savala-Mahany

BALBOA.PRESS
A DIVISION OF HAY HOUSE

Balboa Press books may be ordered through
booksellers or by contacting:

Balboa Press
A Division of Hay House
1663 Liberty Drive
Bloomington, IN 47403
www.balboapress.com
844-682-1282

Print information available on the last page.

ISBN: 979-8-7652-4364-0 (sc)
ISBN: 979-8-7652-4363-3 (e)

Balboa Press rev. date: 11/17/2023

CONTENTS

INTRODUCTION

SETTING THE CONTEXT: THE RISE OF AI AND ITS IMPACT ON SOCIETY.

The term "artificial intelligence" (AI) refers to the process of programming computer systems to carry out activities that would typically require the intelligence of a human, such as visual perception, speech recognition, decision-making, and problem-solving. The rise of AI has transformed society by enabling automation, improving healthcare, revolutionizing transportation, enhancing communication, personalizing experiences, optimizing finance, transforming education, raising ethical concerns, impacting employment, raising privacy and security issues, and creating socioeconomic implications. AI has brought efficiency, innovation, and convenience while also requiring careful consideration of its ethical and societal implications.

Artificial intelligence (AI) has been pivotal in the digitalization of society because it has accelerated the collection, processing, and analysis of massive volumes of data. This has resulted in innovative solutions, streamlined operations, and increased productivity across various sectors. Artificial intelligence has significantly affected many kinds of media, from writing to visual to dimensional. Artificial intelligence-powered technologies, including natural language processing, image and audio recognition, and computer vision, have entirely transformed how we engage with and consume media. With AI, we can process and analyze vast amounts of data quickly, making finding and accessing the information we need more accessible. The use of AI in smartphone technology has increased in recent years. AI-powered personal assistants, such as Siri and Google Assistant, have become a staple of many people's daily lives. AI-powered technologies also improve the user experience and offer more personalized recommendations and services.

The widespread adoption of automation in many fields is one noticeable effect. AI-powered machines and robots have taken over repetitive and mundane tasks, increasing efficiency and productivity. This has reshaped the job market, with some jobs being replaced while new opportunities in AI development and human-AI collaboration have emerged.

In the healthcare sector, AI has revolutionized diagnostics and treatment planning. Large amounts of medical data can be analyzed using machine learning algorithms to help with early disease identification, personalized care, and medication discovery. The healthcare system and patient outcomes could be drastically altered due to this.

AI has greatly influenced transportation. Self-driving cars and autonomous vehicles are becoming a reality, offering the potential for a safer and more efficient ride. AI algorithms help these vehicles navigate and make decisions, reducing accidents caused by human error and improving traffic management.

AI-powered chatbots and virtual assistants have transformed communication. With the help of (NLP)Natural language processing, machines can now understand and answer human questions, paving the way for more individualized customer service and other applications. Algorithms are used for fraud detection, risk assessment, and algorithmic trading. These technologies can process large volumes of data in real-time, enabling more accurate predictions and efficient financial operations.

Artificial intelligence (AI) is used in educational tools and platforms to facilitate individualized instruction. Customized instruction and feedback are the only benefits that adaptive learning systems bring to the classroom. This has the potential to enhance learning outcomes and improve access to education. It has the potential to revolutionize education, offering personalized and individualized teaching and improved learning outcomes. AI can analyze student data and provide real-time feedback to teachers and students, allowing them to adjust their teaching and learning strategies accordingly. The capacity to tailor lessons to each student is a significant advantage of AI in the classroom. Students' data can be examined by AI, which can subsequently create individualized study plans for each student. Using this method could significantly enhance students' effectiveness and interest in their studies. Artificial intelligence has tremendous potential to transform how we think about and deliver higher education. Technology fueled by AI may provide students with immediate responses to their work, keep them on track academically, and offer a more customized and exciting learning environment.

THE IMPORTANCE OF SELF-AWARENESS IN THE AGE OF AI

AI makes self-awareness more vital for individuals and society. Here's why:

1. **Ethical Considerations**: Individuals must have a profound comprehension of their own values, beliefs, and predispositions as AI systems continue to grow and attain more autonomy. Self-awareness allows us to critically evaluate the ethical implications of AI applications and make informed decisions about their development, deployment, and use.
2. **Mitigating Bias:** AI systems are only as unbiased as the data they are trained on. Without self-awareness, individuals may unknowingly contribute to biased datasets or develop AI systems that perpetuate discrimination. By cultivating self-awareness, we can become more conscious of our prejudices and strive

toward developing AI systems that are more equitable and inclusive.

3. **Responsible Use:** Self-awareness enables individuals to recognize the potential impact of AI on various aspects of society, such as employment, privacy, and social interactions. By being aware of these implications, individuals can make responsible choices in how AI is developed, implemented, and regulated, ensuring that it aligns with societal values and priorities.

4. **Adaptability and Lifelong Learning:** The rise of AI is reshaping the job market and requiring individuals to adapt and acquire new skills. Self-awareness plays a vital role in recognizing one's strengths, weaknesses, and areas for growth. It fosters a mindset of continuous learning and personal development, allowing individuals to navigate the changing landscape and remain resilient in the face of AI-driven disruptions.

5. **Human-AI Collaboration**: As AI systems become more integrated into our daily lives, self-awareness helps individuals understand the capabilities and limitations of AI. This understanding facilitates effective collaboration between humans

and AI, where individuals can leverage the strengths of AI while providing the necessary oversight, creativity, and emotional intelligence that machines lack.

6. **Psychological Well-being**: The pervasive presence of AI and automation can lead to concerns about job security, identity, and personal autonomy. Self-awareness helps individuals reflect on their own values, interests, and aspirations, enabling them to navigate these changes and make choices that align with their well-being and fulfilment.

7. **Personal Data Protection:** AI systems rely on vast amounts of personal data to function effectively. Self-awareness empowers individuals to be mindful of their digital footprint, understand their rights regarding data privacy, and take measures to protect their personal information from potential misuse or unauthorized access.

8. **Critical Thinking and Evaluation:** Our capacity to think critically and objectively and analyze the information and outputs created by AI systems is improved when we are self-aware. It helps us question and explore the validity, reliability, and potential biases of AI-generated content, predictions, or recommendations. This is

crucial for avoiding blind reliance on AI and making informed judgments.

9. **Preserving Human Connection and Empathy**: While AI can enhance efficiency and convenience, it lacks the emotional intelligence and empathy inherent to human interactions. Self-awareness helps individuals recognize the value of human connection and the importance of maintaining genuine relationships. It encourages us to prioritize and preserve human-to-human interactions alongside the integration of AI technologies.

10. **Identity and Autonomy**: Self-awareness allows individuals to reflect on their identities, values, and desires. In the age of AI, where personalized experiences and recommendations are prevalent, understanding one's preferences and making conscious choices becomes essential. Self-awareness helps protect individual autonomy and guards against undue influence or manipulation by AI algorithms.

11. **Psychological Impact and Well-being:** The pervasive use of AI and digital technologies can have psychological implications, such as information overload, constant connectivity, or social

comparison. Self-awareness enables individuals to monitor and manage their well-being, set boundaries, and seek balance in their interactions with AI to maintain mental health and overall quality of life.

12. **Adaptation to Technological Advancements:** The rapid pace of technological advancements, including AI, can create uncertainty and disruption. Self-awareness fosters a growth mindset and adaptability, allowing individuals to embrace change, acquire new skills, and navigate the evolving technological landscape with confidence and resilience.

13. **Collaboration and Ethical AI Development:** Self-awareness promotes collaboration among individuals, interdisciplinary teams, and organizations involved in AI development. We can foster diverse perspectives, multidisciplinary approaches, and ethical considerations throughout the AI development lifecycle by acknowledging our limitations and biases.

14. **Regulatory and Policy Considerations**: Self-awareness among policymakers and regulators is crucial for crafting effective policies and regulations concerning AI. It is possible to build informed and balanced

approaches to governance through an understanding of the potential dangers, advantages, and societal impact of AI technology. This will ensure that AI is used responsibly and in the best interest of society.

15. **Continuous Learning and Improvement:** Self-awareness encourages a mindset of continuous learning and improvement in the context of AI. It motivates individuals to stay informed about AI advancements, engage in ongoing education and training, and actively participate in shaping the future of AI through research, innovation, and responsible adoption.

PURPOSE OF THE BOOK: NURTURING SELF-AWARENESS AMIDST AI ADVANCEMENTS

Nurturing self-awareness amidst AI advancements involves developing a deeper understanding of oneself and maintaining a conscious approach to technology. It is crucial to consider our feelings, thoughts, and responses to AI technologies in the age of technology. Taking time for self-reflection and introspection allows us to assess how AI impacts our values, beliefs, and overall well-being. We can cultivate self-awareness by being mindful of our experiences and interactions with AI.

Understanding our values and beliefs is essential when engaging with AI. It helps us evaluate how AI aligns with our aspirations and ethical standards. By reflecting on our values, we can make conscious choices about the technologies we use and support. Continuous learning about AI is crucial for nurturing self-awareness. Staying informed about AI advancements, their capabilities, limitations, and potential biases allows us to critically evaluate AI outputs and make informed decisions. Engaging in discussions, attending workshops, and exploring educational resources can help expand our knowledge.

Developing a critical mindset toward AI is essential. Rather than accepting AI outputs at face value, we should question and evaluate them. This includes considering the data sources, potential biases, and ethical implications. By being skeptical and curious, we can avoid blind reliance on AI and exercise our critical thinking skills. Balancing human connection alongside AI integration is vital. Maintaining genuine relationships and acknowledging the limitations of AI in emotional intelligence and empathy allows us to prioritize human-to-human interactions. By fostering meaningful connections, we can preserve our sense of identity and well-being in the presence of AI.

Ultimately, nurturing self-awareness amidst AI advancements involves:

- Introspection.
- Understanding personal values.
- Continuous learning.
- Critical evaluation of AI outputs.
- Maintaining a balance between human and technological interactions.

By cultivating self-awareness, we can make conscious decisions, navigate ethical challenges, and ensure that AI aligns with our individual and societal well-being.

UNDERSTANDING AI AND ITS SELF-AWARENESS

Understanding AI and its self-awareness involves gaining insights into the nature of artificial intelligence and its ability, or lack thereof, to possess self-awareness.

AI refers to developing and implementing computational systems that can perform tasks traditionally requiring human intelligence. These systems are intended to examine data, recognize trends, and base their choices or forecasts on algorithms and models based on what they discover. However, AI lacks consciousness and subjective experiences characteristic of human self-awareness.

AI systems are built to optimize specific objectives, such as accuracy, efficiency, or cost-effectiveness. They operate within predefined boundaries and are constrained by the data and algorithms used in their training. While AI can exhibit impressive capabilities in areas like image recognition or natural language processing, it does not possess an internal sense of self or the ability to reflect on its existence.

However, it is worth noting that researchers and developers are exploring avenues to create AI systems that exhibit some form of self-awareness. This pursuit involves developing algorithms and architectures that allow AI to monitor and modify its processes, adapt to changing conditions, or recognize its limitations. These efforts aim to enhance AI's capabilities and make it more adaptable and intelligent, but they do not imply the development of accurate self-awareness as experienced by humans.

EXPLAINING THE BASICS OF ARTIFICIAL INTELLIGENCE

Instructing computers to carry out human tasks is known as "artificial intelligence" (AI).

Developing algorithms and models that allow computers to evaluate data, discover patterns, make judgments, and learn from experience is a necessary step in this process.

Data and algorithmic processes are at the heart of artificial intelligence. To train AI models, information must be obtained from various sources, including sensors, databases, and the Internet. An artificial intelligence system's behaviour and decision-making are guided by rules and instructions called algorithms.

There are different types of AI, including:

- **Narrow AI** is designed to carry out particular activities or functions and is sometimes called Weak AI. Examples include voice assistants like Siri or Alexa, recommendation systems, or autonomous vehicles. Narrow AI is focused on excelling in a specific domain but lacks general intelligence.
- **General AI:** This is about the concept of artificial intelligence systems that are capable of understanding, learning, and carrying out any intellectual task that a human being can do. General AI remains an ongoing research and development area and does not currently exist.

AI techniques can be broadly classified into two categories:

Machine learning is an artificially intelligent technology that allows machines to learn from data and evolve without explicit programming. This type of AI is called deep learning.

Supervised, unsupervised, and reinforcement learning are three categories of machine learning algorithms. Machine learning (ML) and deep learning (DL) are both examples of ML. The algorithms for machine learning can be broken down into supervised, unsupervised, and reinforcement learning.

Supervised learning involves training models on labelled data to make predictions or classifications. Unsupervised learning involves discovering patterns or structures in unlabeled data. Reinforcement learning uses a reward system to train models through trial and error.

Deep learning: Artificial neural networks modelled after the human brain's structure and operation are the main subject of this branch of machine learning. The design of deep learning algorithms, commonly called neural networks, uses multiple layers to analyze and extract features from enormous volumes of complex data. Deep learning has achieved remarkable success in image and speech recognition. AI applications span many domains, including healthcare, finance, transportation, and robotics. AI systems have the potential to automate repetitive tasks, provide personalized recommendations, improve decision-making, enhance efficiency, and tackle complex problems. However, it's important to consider ethical and societal implications when developing and deploying AI. Concerns such as bias in data, transparency, privacy, job displacement, and the responsible use of AI are crucial considerations to ensure the technology's benefits are harnessed while minimizing potential risks.

BENEFITS AND CHALLENGES OF AI ADVANCEMENTS

Benefits

1. **Automation and efficiency:** AI technologies automate repetitive and time-consuming tasks, reducing human error and increasing efficiency. This allows individuals and organizations to focus on more complex and value-added activities. Automation can streamline processes, increase productivity, and improve resource allocation. The recruitment process can be automated using a variety of AI-based tools. These tools assist in

relieving employees of tiresome manual labor so they may concentrate on complex tasks like strategy and decision-making. The conversational AI recruiter MYA serves as an illustration of this. This application focuses on scheduling screening and sourcing, two time-consuming recruitment processes. Advanced Machine Learning techniques are used to train MYA, and it also uses Natural Language Processing (NLP) to identify details mentioned during a discussion. Additionally, MYA is responsible for developing candidate profiles, running analytics, and ultimately shortlisting candidates.

2. **Increased Productivity:** Artificial intelligence has become crucial in the business world. It is utilized to manage time- and effort-intensive sophisticated computational tasks. Did you know that 64% of businesses use AI-based solutions to increase productivity and growth? The Legal Robot serves as a perfect example of one such program. I think of it as the Harvey Spectre of the virtual world. This bot works with seasoned legal professionals to understand and assess legal writings, explains legal terms using an AI-based grading system, and applies

machine learning methods, including deep learning and natural language processing. By comparing your contract to others in the same industry, you can also ensure it is standard.

3. **Enhanced Decision-making:** AI systems can process and analyze vast amounts of data, extracting valuable insights and patterns. This enables informed and data-driven decision-making, leading to better outcomes in healthcare diagnosis, financial forecasting, customer personalization, and risk management.

4. **Improved Accuracy and Precision:** Regarding activities like speech recognition, image recognition, and natural language processing, AI algorithms are highly accurate and precise. This has applications in medical diagnostics, quality control, fraud detection, and more, where precision is crucial.

5. **Advanced Problem Solving:** AI techniques like machine learning and deep learning enable AI systems to learn from data and adapt to new situations. This empowers AI to tackle complex problems and find optimal optimization, logistics, scheduling, and resource allocation solutions.

6. **Personalized Experiences:** AI algorithms can analyze user preferences, behaviour, and historical data to provide personalized recommendations and experiences. This is seen in applications like personalized marketing, content recommendation systems, and virtual assistants, enhancing user satisfaction and engagement.

7. **Increased Safety and Risk Mitigation:** AI can be utilized in areas where human safety is paramount, such as autonomous vehicles, industrial automation, and hazardous environments. By replacing or augmenting human involvement in high-risk tasks, AI advancements can reduce the likelihood of accidents and improve overall safety.

8. **Scientific Advancements and Research:** AI plays a crucial role in scientific research by analyzing large datasets, simulating complex scenarios, and uncovering patterns and relationships. Predictive models and algorithms may be helpful in data processing and understanding the potential outcomes of specific trends and strategies. Additionally, AI's strong computing capabilities can speed up the quick processing and analysis of data for research and development that would

have otherwise taken humans too long to examine and grasp. Advancements in areas including genetics, drug discovery, climate modelling, and particle physics have been made possible by AI algorithms.

9. **Accessibility and Inclusion**: AI technologies have the potential to enhance accessibility and inclusion for individuals with disabilities. Voice recognition, assistive technologies, and computer vision applications can enable people with visual or hearing impairments to interact more effectively with technology and the world.

10. **Economic Growth and Innovation:** AI advancements have the potential to drive economic growth and spur innovation. AI-powered technologies create new markets, generate employment opportunities, and foster entrepreneurship. They can transform sectors and promote growth economically.

What are the challenges of AI advancements?

While AI advancements offer numerous benefits, they also present challenges that must be addressed. Here are some key challenges associated with AI advancements:

1. **Ethical Considerations**: Ethical concerns arise as AI becomes more advanced and autonomous. Issues such as AI bias, privacy violations, and the potential for AI to be used for malicious purposes must be addressed. Ensuring fairness, transparency, and accountability in AI algorithms and decision-making processes is essential.

2. **Bias and Discrimination:** AI systems can inherit biases from the training data, leading to biased outcomes and discriminatory behavior. This can result in unfair treatment, perpetuating societal biases and exacerbating inequalities. Efforts must be made to mitigate bias and ensure fairness in AI algorithms and data sets.

3. **Job Displacement and Workforce Changes:** The automation potential of AI raises concerns about job displacement and changes in the workforce. As AI takes over repetitive tasks, job losses in specific sectors are possible. Reskilling and upskilling programs should be implemented to prepare individuals for

the changing job landscape and ensure a smooth transition.

4. **Safety and Security Risks:** AI systems can pose safety and security risks if not adequately designed or protected. Autonomous vehicles, for example, raise concerns about accidents and cybersecurity threats. Ensuring robust safeguards, rigorous testing, and appropriate regulations are essential to mitigate risks and ensure public safety.

5. **Lack of Transparency and Explanability:** Many AI algorithms, particularly those based on deep learning, can be complex and challenging to interpret. This lack of transparency raises concerns about how AI systems reach their decisions. Efforts are being made to develop explainable AI methods to ensure transparency and accountability.

6. **Data Privacy and Security:** AI relies on vast data for training and decision-making. This raises privacy concerns regarding collecting, storing, and using personal data. Strict data protection measures and privacy regulations are necessary to safeguard individuals' privacy rights and prevent data breaches.

7. **Trust and Acceptance:** Building trust and acceptance of AI technologies among users and society is crucial. Misunderstandings, fear, and mistrust can hinder AI adoption and responsible use. Transparent communication, clear guidelines, and addressing public concerns are essential to foster trust in AI systems.

8. **Limited Generalization and Contextual Understanding:** AI systems often struggle to generalize knowledge learned in one context to new situations or understand complex nuances. They may lack common sense reasoning and work with real-world context, limiting their effectiveness in specific tasks and domains.

9. **Legal and Regulatory Frameworks:** The rapid advancement of AI technology has outpaced the development of comprehensive legal and regulatory frameworks. To guarantee the development and deployment of artificial intelligence in a responsible and accountable manner, it is vital to design good rules that address AI's ethical, legal, and social elements.

UNVEILING THE POTENTIAL IMPACT ON HUMAN SELF-AWARENESS AND IDENTITY

Revealing the possible effects on human self-awareness and identity involves recognizing the profound consequences that arise from the integration of advanced technologies, including AI, on how individuals perceive themselves and understand their own identity.

The implementation of AI has the potential to enhance human self-awareness while also bringing new obstacles to human identity. On the one hand, individuals can get a heightened sense of self-awareness as a result of the new insights and information about themselves that can be provided by AI technology. AI-powered tools, for instance, can examine vast volumes of data to recognize patterns and trends in an individual's behaviour, preferences, or health and provide customized feedback and direction.

This increased access to information can deepen individuals' understanding of themselves and foster a more nuanced self-awareness.

The reliance on AI for self-perception and identity formation raises concerns. As individuals engage with AI systems that attempt to analyze and categorize their characteristics, preferences, and behaviours, individuals are likely to define themselves solely based on algorithmic interpretations. This reliance on external technology may lead to a diminished sense of agency and a loss of personal introspection in constructing one's identity.

Moreover, the pervasive use of AI technologies in various aspects of life can blur the boundaries between humans and machines, potentially challenging traditional notions of identity. As AI systems become more sophisticated in mimicking human-like qualities, such as natural language processing or emotional recognition, individuals may encounter situations where it becomes difficult to distinguish between human and AI interactions. This blurring of boundaries can impact how individuals perceive their identity and the nature of human uniqueness.

Another potential impact on self-awareness and identity lies in the possible reinforcement of biases and the shaping of individual perceptions. AI algorithms are trained on large datasets, which may contain societal preconceptions and prejudices. If these biases are not adequately addressed, AI systems can unintentionally perpetuate and amplify existing inequalities, shaping individuals' perceptions of themselves and others. This can result in a distorted self-image and a limited understanding of one's identity, influenced by biased AI systems. The reliance on AI for personalization and decision-making can create filter bubbles and echo chambers, limiting individuals' exposure to diverse perspectives and potentially narrowing their self-awareness. AI systems often recommend content based on past preferences, reinforcing existing beliefs and intentions rather than challenging them. This can limit the exploration of new ideas, experiences, and alternative identities, hindering the development of a more comprehensive self-awareness.

THE SIGNIFICANCE OF SELF-AWARENESS

WHAT SELF-AWARENESS IS

Self-awareness is the ability to recognize, understand, and have conscious knowledge of one's thoughts, feelings, sensations, and behaviors. It involves introspection, reflection, and a deep understanding of one's identity, beliefs, values, and motivations. Self-aware people have a distinct vision of themselves as different persons who exist apart from others, and they are conscious of how their ideas and actions affect not only themselves but those in the world around them.

Self-awareness allows individuals to gain insights into their own experiences, emotions, and reactions, leading to a better understanding of oneself and more intentional and adaptive behaviors.

The role of self-awareness in personal growth and well-being is significant. Here are some critical aspects of its function:

1. **Self-Reflection**: Self-awareness allows individuals to engage in self-reflection, which involves examining one's thoughts, emotions, and behaviors. It helps individuals understand their strengths, weaknesses, values, and beliefs. Self-reflection enables personal growth by identifying areas for improvement and setting goals to enhance oneself.

2. **Emotional Intelligence:** Self-awareness is closely linked to emotional intelligence. It helps people notice and understand their own emotions and those of others. By being self-aware, individuals can regulate their emotions effectively, communicate empathetically, and build healthier relationships.

3. **Authenticity and Self-Expression:** Self-awareness helps individuals discover their authentic selves. It allows individuals to understand their actual values, passions, and interests. With this awareness, individuals can align their actions and decisions with their authentic selves, leading to a sense of purpose, fulfillment, and increased self-esteem.

4. **Effective Communication and Relationships**: Self-awareness enhances interpersonal relationships by facilitating effective communication and empathy. Individuals can better understand and empathize when they know their thoughts, emotions, and biases. This awareness helps build stronger connections, resolve conflicts, and foster healthy relationships.

5. **Personal Responsibility and Accountability:** Self-awareness fosters a sense of personal responsibility and accountability. It enables individuals to recognize the impact of their actions on themselves and others. Self-awareness makes individuals more likely to take ownership of their behaviours, learn from their mistakes, and make positive changes.

6. **Resilience and Adaptability:** Self-awareness helps individuals develop resilience and adaptability. By understanding their strengths, weaknesses, and coping mechanisms, individuals can navigate challenges more effectively and bounce back from setbacks. This resilience contributes to overall well-being and the ability to thrive in various circumstances.

7. **Self-Care and Well-being:** Self-awareness is closely connected to self-care and well-being. When individuals know their physical, emotional, and mental needs, they can prioritize self-care activities that promote their well-being. Self-awareness helps individuals recognize signs of stress, burnout, or imbalance, enabling them to take proactive steps to maintain their well-being.

8. **Goal Setting and Achievement**: Self-awareness helps individuals set meaningful and achievable goals. By understanding their strengths, weaknesses, and values, individuals can set goals that align with their aspirations and motivations. Self-awareness also allows for self-monitoring and adjusting strategies, leading to tremendous success in goal achievement.

9. **Conflict Resolution**: Self-awareness contributes to effective conflict resolution. When individuals know their emotions, triggers, and communication styles, they can engage in constructive dialogue, manage conflicts more skillfully, and find mutually beneficial solutions.

10. **Empowerment and Agency**: Self-awareness empowers individuals to take control of their lives. They can then take proactive steps to address any patterns, habits, or behaviours preventing them from moving forward. Self-awareness helps individuals develop a sense of agency, enabling them to make choices that align with their values and aspirations.

EXPLORING THE BENEFITS OF SELF-AWARENESS IN NAVIGATING AI-INFUSED ENVIRONMENTS

Exploring the benefits of self-awareness in navigating AI-infused environments involves recognizing how cultivating self-awareness empowers individuals to make informed decisions, maintain autonomy, and navigate the complexities of AI-driven technologies effectively. In AI-infused environments, where artificial intelligence is pervasive, self-awareness plays a crucial role in several ways.

- Self-awareness allows individuals to critically evaluate the information and recommendations provided by AI systems. By being aware of their own values, beliefs, and goals, individuals can assess whether AI-driven suggestions align with their personal preferences and make choices accordingly.
- Self-awareness enables individuals to recognize and manage potential biases in AI technologies. AI algorithms are developed based on large datasets, and if these datasets contain biases, the algorithms may perpetuate them. With self-awareness, individuals can become mindful of their own biases and actively seek to challenge and address any biases they encounter in AI systems, promoting fairness and inclusivity.
- Self-awareness helps individuals maintain a sense of agency and control over their interactions with AI. By being aware of their own needs, boundaries, and limits, individuals can set appropriate boundaries with AI technologies, ensuring that their personal privacy and autonomy are

respected. Self-awareness empowers individuals to make deliberate choices about when and how to engage with AI, avoiding over-reliance or dependency.

- Self-awareness fosters adaptability and learning in AI-infused environments. By understanding their own strengths, weaknesses, and learning styles, individuals can leverage AI tools to enhance their learning and personal growth effectively. Self-awareness allows individuals to identify areas where AI can support their development, whether through personalized learning recommendations, skill-building resources, or feedback.

- Self-awareness helps individuals maintain a balanced perspective and emotional well-being in AI-infused environments. By being attuned to their own emotions and mental state, individuals can gauge how AI technologies impact their well-being. This awareness allows individuals to adjust their usage, seek alternative sources of support or validation, and ensure that their emotional health is not compromised by excessive reliance on AI-driven interactions.

- Self-awareness facilitates the responsible and ethical use of AI. With a deep understanding of their values and ethical principles, individuals can actively consider the broader implications of AI technologies. By reflecting on the ethical considerations surrounding privacy, data security, fairness, and transparency, individuals can advocate for responsible AI development and usage, promoting positive societal impact.

- One significant benefit is the ability to maintain authenticity and individuality. In AI-infused environments, where AI systems strive to personalize experiences and cater to individual preferences, self-awareness helps individuals discern their true desires and values. By being self-aware, individuals can resist conforming to AI-generated suggestions that may not align with their genuine interests, allowing them to stay true to themselves.

- Self-awareness also enhances critical thinking and decision-making abilities. In an environment where AI systems provide recommendations and automate certain tasks, being self-aware enables individuals to evaluate the reasoning behind AI-driven suggestions. By questioning, analyzing, and reflecting on these recommendations, individuals can make informed decisions, leveraging the benefits of AI while retaining their cognitive autonomy.

- Self-awareness also promotes resilience and adaptability. As AI technologies evolve rapidly, individuals who possess self-awareness can more easily adapt to new tools, platforms, and changes in AI systems. They can recognize their own learning preferences and embrace opportunities to acquire new AI-related skills, effectively adapting to the evolving landscape and leveraging AI advancements to their advantage.

- self-awareness facilitates effective collaboration and teamwork in AI-infused environments. By understanding their own strengths, weaknesses, and communication styles, individuals can contribute meaningfully to multidisciplinary teams that develop or utilize AI technologies. Self-awareness helps individuals navigate the complexities of collaborative work, fostering better cooperation, understanding, and synergy within diverse AI-focused teams.

EXAMINING THE POTENTIAL CONSEQUENCES OF NEGLECTING

SELF-AWARENESS AMIDST AI ADVANCEMENTS

Examining the potential consequences of neglecting self-awareness amidst AI advancements involves understanding the risks and implications that arise when individuals fail to prioritize and nurture their own self-awareness in the face of rapid technological progress. As AI technologies become more prevalent and integrated into various aspects of our lives, there is a risk of losing touch with our inner selves and becoming disconnected from our thoughts, emotions, values, and aspirations. Neglecting self-awareness in this context can lead to several detrimental consequences.

One consequence is the erosion of personal agency. When individuals lack self-awareness, they may become passive recipients of AI-driven recommendations, decisions, and behaviors. They may rely heavily on algorithms and automated systems, foregoing their own critical thinking and decision-making processes. This can result in a diminished sense of personal autonomy and a reduced ability to make choices aligned with one's values and aspirations.

Another consequence is the potential for AI-driven manipulation. Without self-awareness, individuals may be more susceptible to manipulation by AI systems designed to exploit their vulnerabilities, preferences, or biases. A lack of self-awareness can make it difficult to recognize and challenge the biases embedded in AI algorithms, leading to the potential reinforcement of harmful stereotypes, discrimination, or misinformation. Neglecting self-awareness can also hinder personal growth and development. Self-awareness is a crucial foundation for introspection, learning, and self-improvement. It allows individuals to understand their strengths, weaknesses, and areas for growth. By neglecting self-awareness, individuals may miss out on opportunities for personal growth, as they fail to recognize their own limitations or areas that require attention and development.

Furthermore, neglecting self-awareness amidst AI advancements can impact mental and emotional well-being. Self-awareness enables individuals to recognize and regulate their emotions, manage stress, and nurture their overall psychological health. Without self-awareness, individuals may become disconnected from their own emotions and experiences, leading to increased stress, anxiety, or a diminished sense of fulfillment. Society as a whole may also face consequences when self-awareness is neglected in the context of AI advancements.

Without self-awareness, individuals may adopt a passive stance toward the ethical and societal implications of AI. They may fail to critically evaluate the potential biases, privacy concerns, or social implications associated with AI technologies. This can hinder progress toward responsible and inclusive AI development and deployment.

EMBRACING MINDFULNESS AND REFLECTION

INTRODUCING MINDFULNESS PRACTICES FOR DEVELOPING SELF-AWARENESS

Mindfulness is the practice of intentionally paying attention to the present moment without judgment. It involves bringing awareness to our thoughts, emotions, bodily sensations, and the surrounding environment. Rather than being caught up in the past or worrying about the future, mindfulness encourages us to fully experience and engage with the present moment.

At its core, mindfulness involves cultivating a non-judgmental and accepting attitude toward our experiences. It allows us to observe our thoughts and emotions as they arise, without getting entangled in them or labeling them as good or bad. Through mindfulness, we develop a greater sense of clarity, presence, and self-awareness. Mindfulness can be practiced in various ways, such as through seated meditation, mindful breathing exercises, body scans, or mindful movement practices like yoga. It can be done formally, by setting aside dedicated time for practice, as well as informally by incorporating mindfulness into our daily activities.

The benefits of mindfulness are wide-ranging. It has been shown to reduce stress, enhance focus and attention, improve emotional regulation, increase resilience, and promote overall well-being. By developing mindfulness, we cultivate a deeper understanding of ourselves, our patterns of thinking and reacting, and our relationship with the world around us. Practicing mindfulness requires patience and commitment. It is a skill that can be developed over time through regular practice and gentle perseverance. Whether you are new to mindfulness or have been practicing for a while, it offers a valuable tool for self-discovery, personal growth, and navigating the complexities of life, including AI-infused environments.

Introducing mindfulness practices for developing self-awareness can be done in a gradual and personalized manner. Here's a step-by-step approach you can follow:

1. **Understand the Basics:** Familiarize yourself with the concept of mindfulness and its benefits. Educate yourself about the various mindfulness techniques and approaches available. . Read books, and articles, or watch videos on the topic to gain a deeper understanding of mindfulness practices and their role in self-awareness.

2. **Personal Commitment**: Make a personal commitment to prioritize self-awareness and mindfulness in your life. Recognize the value of self-awareness and its potential impact on personal growth and well-being.

3. **Start Small:** Begin with short and manageable mindfulness sessions. Start with just a few minutes each day and gradually increase the duration as you become more comfortable. Consistency is key, so aim for regular practice.

4. **Choose a Technique**: Explore different mindfulness techniques to find one that

resonates with you. Options include mindful breathing, body scans, guided meditations, or mindful movement practices like yoga or walking. Experiment and find what works best for you.

5. **Create a Dedicated Space:** Set aside a quiet and comfortable space where you can practice mindfulness without distractions. This space can help create a sense of calm and focus during your mindfulness sessions.

6. **Set a Routine:** Establish a routine for your mindfulness practice. Decide on a specific time of day when you can dedicate uninterrupted time for mindfulness. It can be in the morning, during a lunch break, or in the evening—whatever suits your schedule best.

7. **Seek Guidance**: Consider attending mindfulness classes, workshops, or retreats to receive guidance from experienced teachers. They can provide instruction, and support, and answer any questions you may have as you begin your mindfulness journey.

8. **Utilize Apps or Online Resources:** Explore mindfulness apps or online resources that offer guided meditations, mindfulness exercises, or helpful tools to

support your practice. These resources can provide structure and guidance, especially if you're new to mindfulness.

9. **Integrate Mindfulness into Daily Life**: Extend mindfulness beyond formal practice. Apply mindfulness to everyday activities like eating, walking, or engaging in conversations. Cultivate an attitude of presence, curiosity, and non-judgment in all aspects of your life.

10. **Patience and Kindness:** Remember that developing self-awareness takes time and patience. Be kind to yourself throughout the process and embrace any challenges or distractions that arise during your mindfulness practice. Approach yourself and your experiences with gentleness and compassion.

By following these steps, you can introduce mindfulness practices into your life, creating a foundation for developing self-awareness. As you continue to cultivate mindfulness, you'll gradually enhance your ability to observe your thoughts, emotions, and experiences, leading to a deeper understanding of yourself and your interactions with AI-infused environments.

CULTIVATING REFLECTION AS A TOOL FOR UNDERSTANDING ONESELF IN THE DIGITAL AGE

Cultivating reflection as a tool for understanding oneself in the digital age involves intentionally creating opportunities for introspection and self-examination amidst the pervasive influence of technology. We live in an age where information, notifications, and distractions from our numerous digital devices are continuously barraging us. This continuous influx of stimuli can hinder our ability to pause, reflect, and gain a deeper understanding of ourselves. Thus, it becomes crucial to cultivate the practice of reflection as a means of self-exploration and self-awareness.

Reflection involves time and space for contemplation, introspection, and evaluation of our thoughts, emotions, and experiences. We should take a break from our constant online activity to reflect alone.

In the digital age, reflection can be facilitated through various approaches. For instance,

- journaling or writing can serve as a reflective tool, allowing us to capture and examine our thoughts, insights, and personal narratives. An essay provides an opportunity to explore our inner world, clarify our values, and identify patterns or areas for growth.

- Engaging in mindfulness practices can also enhance reflection. Mindfulness includes consciously focusing on the present and non-judgmentally noticing thoughts and feelings. By cultivating mindfulness, we can better understand our internal landscape, recognize automatic reactions, and make conscious choices aligned with our values.

- Creating solitude and quiet reflection space is essential in the digital age. Disconnecting from digital devices and embracing solitude allows us to connect with our inner selves, enabling deeper introspection and self-discovery. Walking in the woods, focusing on a hobby, or sitting quietly are all great ways to do this.

- Engaging in meaningful conversations and seeking diverse perspectives can also foster reflection. Engaging with others with different experiences, beliefs, and backgrounds challenges our assumptions and expands our understanding of ourselves and the world. Meaningful conversations provide opportunities for self-reflection by prompting us to articulate and refine our thoughts and beliefs.

By cultivating reflection as a tool for self-understanding in the digital age, we can navigate the complexities of modern life while maintaining a solid sense of self. Meditation enables us to uncover our values, aspirations, and purpose, allowing us to make intentional choices and live authentically in a technology-driven world.

BALANCING TECHNOLOGY USE WITH MINDFUL PRESENCE AND SELF-REFLECTION

Balancing technology use with mindful presence and self-reflection involves finding a harmonious equilibrium between engaging with technology and fostering moments of conscious awareness and introspection.

In today's digital age, technology is deeply integrated into our lives, offering constant connectivity, information access, and entertainment. However, excessive reliance on technology can lead to a diminished sense of presence and a lack of self-reflection. Therefore, it becomes essential to cultivate a balanced approach.

Mindful presence involves fully engaging in the present moment and being consciously aware of one's thoughts, emotions, and surroundings.

It requires intentionally directing attention to the current experience rather than being absorbed by technology-driven distractions. By practicing mindfulness, individuals can develop a deeper connection with themselves, their environment, and the people around them.

Self-reflection complements mindful presence by encouraging introspection and understanding of one's thoughts, emotions, and actions. It involves pausing, contemplating, and evaluating personal experiences, values, and goals. Self-reflection helps individuals gain insights, make meaning from their experiences, and align their behaviors and choices with their authentic selves.

Balancing technology use with mindful presence, and self-reflection entails integrating intentional practices into daily routines. It involves setting boundaries and creating designated periods of uninterrupted self-reflection, introspection, and quality face-to-face interactions. Disconnecting from technology periodically allows individuals to reconnect with their inner selves and engage in activities that nurture personal growth, creativity, and well-being. Meditation, deep breathing, and sensory awareness can improve present-moment awareness. By consciously noticing and appreciating the simple joys of life, individuals can counterbalance the constant stimulation provided by technology and develop a greater sense of well-being.

Furthermore, fostering self-reflection involves journaling, engaging in meaningful conversations, or seeking solitude for introspection. These practices encourage individuals to explore their thoughts, emotions, and values, fostering self-awareness and personal growth. Through self-reflection, individuals can evaluate their relationship with technology and make conscious choices about its usage.

UNPLUGGING AND RECONNECTING WITH THE SELF

Unplugging and reconnecting with the self refers to the intentional act of disconnecting from external distractions, such as technology or the demands of daily life, to focus on and nurture one's inner self. In today's fast-paced and digitally connected world, constant exposure to technology and external stimuli can often lead to overwhelming stress and disconnection from one's thoughts, emotions, and values. Unplugging involves deliberately stepping away from technology and creating dedicated periods to engage in activities that promote self-reflection, self-care, and a deeper understanding of oneself.

By unplugging, individuals can create space for introspection and self-awareness. Journaling, meditation, and mindfulness help you express yourself and have fun. Unplugging allows individuals to tune into their thoughts and emotions, gaining a clearer perspective on their desires, values, and aspirations.

Reconnecting with the self also involves nurturing one's physical, emotional, and mental well-being. Exercise, nature, thankfulness, and creativity are self-care activities. It entails prioritizing one's own needs and taking the time to rejuvenate and replenish personal energy reserves.

Unplugging and reconnecting with the self can have several benefits.

- It can help individuals reduce stress, improve focus and productivity, enhance creativity, and foster inner peace and fulfillment. By disconnecting from external distractions and prioritizing self-care, individuals can cultivate a stronger connection with their authentic selves, leading to a deeper understanding of their values, beliefs, and life purpose.

- Unplugging allows individuals to establish healthier boundaries with technology and find a healthier balance. It encourages mindful technology use and conscious time allocation for self-reflection and self-care. By consciously choosing when and how to engage with technology, individuals can create a more intentional and fulfilling relationship with it rather than being overwhelmed or controlled by it.

RECOGNIZING THE NEED FOR DIGITAL DETOX AND SETTING HEALTHY BOUNDARIES

Recognizing the need for a digital detox and setting healthy limits involves admitting the possible negative impact of excessive use of technology and taking proactive efforts to create a healthier and more balanced relationship with digital devices and online activities. This can be accomplished by recognizing the potential negative impact of excessive use of technology and creating healthy boundaries. Technology has quickly become an inseparable component of our life, bringing many advantages and luxuries. However, excessive or uncontrolled use of technology can lead to decreased productivity, reduced focus, sleep disturbances, social isolation, and heightened stress levels. Recognizing these potential consequences is the first step towards acknowledging the need for a digital detox.

Digital detox is a deliberate break from technology and the internet. This break allows individuals to recharge, rejuvenate, and regain balance. It involves setting boundaries and consciously reducing or eliminating technology use during designated periods or activities.

Setting healthy boundaries with technology involves establishing guidelines for how and when digital devices are used. This can include:

- **Designating device-free zones or times:** Setting specific areas or periods where technology is not allowed, such as during meals, before bed, or in certain house rooms. This promotes focused attention on other activities and enhances interpersonal connections.
- **Implementing screen-free routines:** Creating activities that do not include using a screen, such as going to the gym, pursuing passions, connecting with family or self-care, may help. These activities provide an opportunity for relaxation,

creativity, and personal growth away from digital distractions.

- **Practicing mindful technology use**: Being intentional and present while using technology, rather than mindlessly scrolling or engaging in excessive multitasking. It involves being aware of the impact of technology on one's well-being and consciously choosing how to engage with it.
- **Limiting notifications and distractions**: Adjust device settings to minimize unnecessary notifications and interruptions. This helps reduce the constant pull of digital distractions and promotes focused attention on important tasks or meaningful interactions.

Recognizing the need for a digital detox and setting healthy boundaries with technology can have numerous benefits. It allows individuals to reclaim their time and attention, improve focus and productivity, enhance mental well-being, strengthen relationships, and foster a greater sense of balance in life. It's important to remember that digital detox and setting boundaries with technology are individual choices. The specific approach may vary for each person based on their lifestyle, responsibilities, and preferences.

Individuals can establish a healthier relationship with digital devices and prioritize their overall well-being by finding the right balance between technology use and disconnection.

REDISCOVERING ANALOG EXPERIENCES AND RECONNECTING WITH THE PHYSICAL WORLD

Rediscovering analog experiences and reconnecting with the physical world involves intentionally seeking out and engaging in activities that do not rely on digital technology, allowing individuals to reconnect with their surroundings' tangible and sensory aspects. In an increasingly digital and technology-driven society, many experiences have become mediated through screens and virtual platforms. Rediscovering analog experiences involves embracing activities that involve physical objects, face-to-face interactions, and direct engagement with the environment.

Engaging in analog experiences can include:

- **Reading physical books:** Instead of consuming digital content, reading physical books allows for a tactile experience, the feel of turning pages, and the opportunity to immerse oneself in the written word without the distractions of screens.

- **Writing with pen and paper:** Opting for handwritten notes, journals, or letters brings a tangible and personal touch to communication and self-expression. It allows for a slower and more deliberate form of writing that can enhance creativity and reflection.
- **Exploring nature:** Spending time outdoors, whether walking in the park, hiking, or gardening, allows individuals to connect with the natural world. Engaging with nature stimulates the senses, promotes mindfulness, and provides a break from the digital realm.
- **Engaging in arts and crafts**: Painting, drawing, knitting, or woodworking offer a hands-on and creative experience. Working with physical materials provides a sense of accomplishment and a connection with the creation process.
- **Socializing face-to-face:** Prioritizing in-person interactions with friends, family, and colleagues fosters deeper connections and meaningful conversations. It allows for nonverbal cues, shared experiences, and a sense of presence that can be more fulfilling than digital communication.

Rediscovering analog experiences and reconnecting with the physical world offers numerous benefits. It can enhance mindfulness, reduce stress, improve creativity, foster deeper connections with others, and provide a sense of grounding and balance in an increasingly digital and fast-paced society. By intentionally carving out time for analog experiences, individuals can cultivate a greater appreciation for the sensory aspects of life, reestablish a connection with the physical world, and find moments of respite from the constant digital stimulation.

FOSTERING GENUINE HUMAN CONNECTIONS AMIDST THE PREVALENCE OF AI-DRIVEN INTERACTIONS

Fostering genuine human connections amidst the prevalence of AI-driven interactions involves actively nurturing meaningful relationships, emphasizing empathy, and prioritizing authentic interpersonal relations in a world where technology and AI are increasingly shaping our interactions. As AI-driven interactions become more prevalent, such as automated customer service or virtual assistants, there is a risk of losing the human touch and the depth of connection from genuine human interactions. To counteract this, it is essential to focus on:

1. **Emphasizing empathy and emotional intelligence:** Developing and practicing empathy allows individuals to understand and connect with others more deeply. It involves listening, understanding, and responding with genuine care and concern. Individuals can navigate complex emotions and establish more meaningful connections with others by cultivating emotional intelligence.

2. **Active listening and presence:** Being fully present and attentive during conversations is essential for fostering genuine connections. Actively listening, engaging in meaningful dialogue, and showing genuine interest in other's perspectives and experiences contribute to deeper relationships and a sense of being honestly heard and understood.

3. **Balancing technology use:** While technology can facilitate communication and connections, finding a healthy balance is essential. Setting boundaries for technology use and being mindful of the quality of our interactions can help ensure that we allocate sufficient time

and energy to nurturing genuine human connections.

4. **Engaging in shared activities and experiences:** Participating in activities or hobbies can create shared memories and strengthen connections. Engaging in collaborative projects, going on outings, or pursuing mutual interests fosters a sense of belonging and strengthens bonds with others.

5. **Cultivating vulnerability and authenticity:** Being open and vulnerable in our interactions allows for deeper connections. Communicating our thoughts, feelings, and experiences can foster trust, understanding, and genuine human relationships.

We can ensure that technology acts as a tool to improve, rather than replace, authentic relationships if we intentionally prioritize genuine human connections and remain sensitive to the possible limitations of AI-driven interactions. This will enable efficient technology use. Nurturing empathy, engaging in face-to-face interactions, active listening, and embracing vulnerability can foster more profound and meaningful connections in the face of AI-driven interactions.

NAVIGATING ETHICAL DILEMMAS AND DECISION-MAKING

Navigating ethical dilemmas and decision-making involves carefully considering the potential consequences of our actions, weighing different ethical frameworks, and making choices that align with our values and principles. Ethical dilemmas arise when conflicting moral principles or choices require us to make difficult decisions. To navigate these dilemmas:

Identify and define the ethical dilemma: Clearly describe the conflicting values or possibilities at play, and ensure you understand how the decision may impact the various stakeholders.

Gather information and perspectives: Seek relevant information, facts, and viewpoints from different sources. Consider all of the ideas and viewpoints that those people who may have their lives affected by the choice may have.

Evaluate ethical frameworks: Familiarize yourself with different ethical theories and frameworks, such as utilitarianism, deontology, virtue ethics, or principles of justice. Reflect on how these frameworks align with your values and principles.

Reflect on consequences and long-term impact: Consider each course of action's potential outcomes and consequences. Determine the immediate and long-term repercussions on people, communities, the environment, and society.

Seek guidance and engage in dialogue: Consult with trusted mentors, colleagues, or experts who can provide insights and guidance on the ethical dilemma. Engage in thoughtful discussions and debates to gain different perspectives and challenge your assumptions.

Take responsibility and make an informed decision: In the end, you have to decide after carefully weighing the evidence, moral values, and the potential effects on diverse stakeholders. Strive to make a decision that aligns with your values and contributes to the greater good.

Reflect and learn from the experience: Reflect on the outcomes and consequences after deciding. Evaluate whether the decision aligned with your ethical reasoning and values. Learn from the experience to inform future ethical decision-making.

DISCUSSING THE ETHICAL CONSIDERATIONS SURROUNDING AI TECHNOLOGIES

Ethical considerations surrounding AI technologies revolve around the potential impact of AI systems on various aspects of society, including privacy, bias and discrimination, accountability, transparency, and the future of work. These considerations ensure that AI is developed, deployed, and used responsibly and ethically. Here are some key ethical considerations:

1. **Bias and Fairness:** AI systems can reflect and perpetuate biases present in the data used to train them, leading to discriminatory outcomes. It is crucial

to ensure fairness, transparency, and accountability in AI algorithms, addressing issues related to race, gender, age, and other protected characteristics.

2. **Privacy and Security**: Artificial intelligence systems frequently rely on enormous volumes of personal data, raising worries about the breach of privacy and data security. The sensitive information of individuals needs to be protected by having safeguards in place to prevent unauthorized access or misuse of the information.

3. **Responsibility and Accountability**: Determining accountability for AI decisions can be challenging, especially when complex systems are involved. Establishing clear lines of responsibility, liability, and oversight is essential to address potential harm caused by AI applications.

4. **Human Autonomy and Control**: AI should be developed and deployed in a way that respects and enhances human autonomy. Decisions made by AI systems should be subject to human control and should not undermine individuals' freedom, privacy, or dignity.

5. **Impact on Employment**: The automation potential of AI raises concerns about job displacement and socioeconomic inequalities. Ethical considerations include:
   - Mitigating the adverse effects on workers.
   - Retraining programs.
   - Ensuring equitable distribution of benefits derived from AI advancements.

6. **Transparency and Explainability:** AI systems should provide understandable and explainable reasoning for their decisions and actions. This promotes trust, facilitates error detection, and enables individuals to challenge or contest outcomes that may affect them.

7. **Safety and Risk Mitigation**: AI technologies can have significant impacts, and assessing and mitigating potential risks and unintended consequences is crucial. This includes ensuring robust testing, validation, and safeguards against adversarial attacks or unintended system behaviors.

8. **Informed Consent:** Obtaining informed consent becomes crucial when AI systems process personal data or make decisions with potential consequences.

People should be able to understand and have some control over how AI-enabled activities that affect them come out, and they should be aware of how their data is being used.

9. **Global Considerations:** AI technologies transcend borders, and ethical considerations should extend to international collaborations and applications. Standards and guidelines should be developed globally, considering cultural, social, and legal differences.

10. **Long-term Implications**: Ethical deliberations surrounding AI should extend beyond immediate concerns and consider potential long-term implications. This includes considerations about the impact on social structures, power dynamics, and the potential for AI to shape or influence societal values.

Addressing these ethical considerations requires a multidisciplinary approach involving technologists, ethicists, policymakers, and the broader society to ensure that AI technologies are developed and deployed to promote human well-being, fairness, and societal benefits.

EXAMINING THE IMPACT OF AI ON PERSONAL VALUES AND DECISION-MAKING PROCESSES

Examining the impact of AI on personal values and decision-making processes involves a comprehensive analysis of how AI technologies can shape, influence, or even challenge our values and the way we make decisions. Here are some key points to consider:

Value Alignment: AI systems operate based on predefined objectives and criteria, which may reflect specific values. When AI influences decision-making, it questions how well these values align with personal or societal values. The extent to which AI systems prioritize and incorporate diverse values is essential to assess.

Autonomy and Agency: AI technologies can impact personal freedom and agency by augmenting or replacing decision-making processes. This raises concerns about the degree of control individuals have over decisions made by AI systems and the potential consequences for personal autonomy and agency.

Ethical Dilemmas: AI algorithms may encounter ethical dilemmas when making decisions. These dilemmas can arise from conflicting objectives or value trade-offs. Examining how AI systems navigate these dilemmas and the implications for personal values is crucial.

Bias and Fairness: AI systems can perpetuate biases in the training data, leading to unfair outcomes. Examining the impact of biased algorithms on decision-making processes helps identify potential conflicts with personal values and societal notions of fairness.

Information Filtering and Influence: AI algorithms play a role in filtering and personalizing the information individuals receive. This can influence decision-making by selectively presenting specific perspectives or reinforcing existing beliefs. It is essential to examine how AI technologies shape the information landscape and its impact on personal values.

Trust and Reliance: Trust in AI systems can significantly impact decision-making. Individuals may rely on AI-generated recommendations or judgments, potentially altering their decision-making processes. Understanding the role of trust in AI and its effect on personal values is essential.

Responsibility and Accountability: Determining responsibility and accountability for AI-generated decisions is complex. Examining who is ultimately responsible for the outcomes and potential consequences for personal values helps address accountability and potential harm concerns.

Value Trade-offs: AI systems may need to make value trade-offs when faced with conflicting objectives or ethical dilemmas. Decisions made by AI algorithms can reflect specific values over others, potentially challenging personal values or introducing ethical conflicts.

Ethical Decision-making Frameworks: Developing ethical decision-making frameworks for AI systems becomes crucial to ensure alignment with personal values. Incorporating ethical principles, such as fairness, transparency, and human well-being, into the design and deployment of AI can help mitigate the impact on personal values.

Cultural and Contextual Sensitivity: AI technologies are deployed in diverse cultural and societal contexts. Understanding and respecting cultural variations in values and decision-making processes is essential to prevent the imposition of biased or inappropriate values through AI systems.

Evolving Values: As AI technologies advance, societal values may develop in response to their impact. The ongoing examination of AI's influence on personal values and decision-making processes requires constant reflection, dialogue, and adaptation to ensure that AI aligns with the changing values of individuals and societies.

These considerations highlight the need for interdisciplinary collaboration involving ethicists, technologists, policymakers, and individuals to navigate the complex interplay between AI and personal values, ensuring that AI technologies are developed and deployed to respect and enhance human agency, autonomy, and values.

DEVELOPING ETHICAL FRAMEWORKS AND GUIDELINES FOR ALIGNING AI ADVANCEMENTS WITH PERSONAL VALUES

Developing ethical frameworks and guidelines for aligning AI advancements with personal values is crucial to ensure that AI technologies are designed and deployed to respect and enhance individual values. Here are vital considerations for such frameworks:

Inclusivity and Diversity: Ethical frameworks should prioritize inclusivity and account for diverse personal values across different cultures, communities, and individuals. They should avoid imposing a narrow set of values and instead accommodate a wide range of perspectives.

Value Reflection and Transparency: Ethical

frameworks should emphasize the reflection of personal values in AI systems. Developers should aim for transparency by clearly articulating the values embedded in the algorithms and making them accessible to users.

User Empowerment: Ethical frameworks should promote user empowerment, allowing individuals to understand and shape AI systems' values and decision-making processes. This can be achieved through user interfaces that control, customize, and explain how AI decisions align with personal values.

Value Alignment Assessments: Developers should conduct assessments to evaluate the alignment of AI systems with personal values. These assessments can involve user feedback, stakeholder engagement, and ongoing dialogue to ensure continuous improvement and adaptation.

Informed Consent: Ethical frameworks should incorporate mechanisms to obtain informed consent from individuals whose data is used or whose decisions are influenced by AI systems. Individuals should have the right to understand how their values are being considered and the ability to opt-out or modify the system's behavior.

Accountability and Redress: Ethical frameworks should define mechanisms for accountability and redress in cases where AI systems diverge from personal values or cause harm. This includes clear lines of responsibility, complaint and dispute resolution avenues, and mechanisms for correcting or modifying AI behavior.

Multi-Stakeholder Collaboration: Developing ethical frameworks should involve collaboration among technologists, ethicists, policymakers, and representatives of diverse user groups. This interdisciplinary approach helps ensure that various perspectives are considered and that ethical considerations are robustly addressed.

Continuous Evaluation and Auditing: Ethical frameworks should encourage ongoing evaluation and auditing of AI systems to assess their alignment with personal values. This involves monitoring the impact on individuals, conducting regular ethics reviews, and addressing emerging issues as AI technologies evolve.

Education and Awareness: Ethical frameworks should promote education and awareness about AI technologies, their capabilities, and their impact on personal values. This empowers individuals to make informed decisions and shape AI systems to align with their values.

Ethical Review Boards: Establishing independent ethical review boards can provide oversight and guidance in developing and deploying AI technologies. These boards can ensure compliance with ethical frameworks, address potential conflicts of interest, and help safeguard personal values.

By developing and adhering to these ethical frameworks and guidelines, we can foster the alignment of AI advancements with personal values, promoting the responsible and beneficial use of AI technologies in a way that respects individual autonomy, diversity, and societal well-being.

HARNESSING AI FOR PERSONAL GROWTH

H arnessing AI for personal growth involves using artificial intelligence technologies to support and empower individuals in their personal development. It means leveraging AI's data analysis, pattern recognition, and prediction capabilities to provide personalized recommendations for health, fitness, learning, productivity, and emotional well-being. By utilizing AI tools and algorithms, individuals can receive tailored guidance, feedback, and interventions to enhance their self-awareness, well-being, and overall growth.

EXPLORING AI TOOLS AND TECHNOLOGIES THAT CAN SUPPORT SELF-AWARENESS

Exploring AI tools and technologies that can support self-awareness involves investigating the various applications of artificial intelligence in promoting introspection and self-understanding. It examines how AI can analyze and interpret personal data, emotions, and experiences to facilitate self-reflection. These AI tools can engage in conversational interactions, analyze language and sentiment, and provide insights and feedback to aid individuals in gaining a deeper understanding of themselves. By leveraging AI, individuals can access innovative approaches to enhance their self-awareness and personal growth.

AI tools can leverage natural language processing and sentiment analysis to analyze written or spoken language, allowing individuals to express their thoughts, emotions, and experiences. Through conversational interactions with AI-powered chatbots or virtual assistants, individuals can engage in self-dialogue, articulate their feelings, and gain insights into their perspectives.

Moreover, AI can assist in identifying patterns and trends in personal data, such as daily routines, habits, and behaviors. By analyzing this data, AI algorithms can provide individuals with objective feedback and visualizations highlighting areas for self-improvement or areas of strength. This feedback can help individuals better understand their own tendencies, enabling them to make more informed decisions and choices aligned with their goals and values.

AI can also contribute to emotional well-being by offering personalized interventions and support. AI-powered systems can detect emotional states through facial expression analysis, voice tone recognition, or physiological signals. Based on these insights, AI can provide tailored recommendations, techniques, or resources to manage stress, enhance relaxation, or improve emotional resilience. AI-driven learning platforms can facilitate personalized learning experiences, catering to individual learning styles and preferences. Adaptive learning algorithms can analyze personal performance data, identify knowledge gaps, and suggest customized learning paths. This enables individuals to develop self-awareness regarding their strengths, weaknesses, and areas of interest and encourages a lifelong learning mindset.

MAXIMIZING THE POTENTIAL OF AI IN ENHANCING PERSONAL WELL-BEING AND SELF-AWARENESS

Maximizing the potential of AI in enhancing personal well-being and self-awareness involves utilizing artificial intelligence technologies to support and empower individuals in various aspects of their lives.

AI can play a significant role in enhancing personal well-being by leveraging its data analysis, pattern recognition, and prediction capabilities. With access to vast amounts of data, AI can assist individuals in making more informed decisions about their health, fitness, and overall lifestyle. It can analyze personal health records, genetic information, and real-time sensor data to provide personalized nutrition, exercise, and preventive measures recommendations. By considering individual preferences, AI algorithms can suggest tailored strategies to improve physical and mental well-being.

AI can contribute to self-awareness by facilitating personal reflection and introspection. Through natural language processing and sentiment analysis, AI-powered tools can help individuals articulate their thoughts, emotions, and experiences, fostering self-expression and self-understanding. Virtual assistants and chatbots can engage in conversational interactions, offering guidance and support and even providing therapeutic interventions for emotional well-being.

AI can also enable personalized learning and self-improvement. Adaptive learning systems can tailor educational content based on individual strengths, weaknesses, and learning styles, optimizing understanding and promoting intellectual growth. AI-powered feedback mechanisms can provide insights into performance and progress, fostering self-assessment and motivation.

Additionally, AI can enhance personal productivity and time management. Intelligent algorithms can analyze work patterns, prioritize tasks, and suggest optimized schedules, enabling individuals to allocate their time effectively and achieve a better work-life balance. AI-powered productivity tools can automate routine tasks, freeing time for meaningful and fulfilling activities.

MINDFUL PARENTING AND EDUCATING IN THE AI ERA

ADDRESSING THE ROLE OF PARENTS AND EDUCATORS IN NURTURING SELF-AWARENESS

In the AI era, parents and educators have become even more critical in cultivating self-awareness in individuals. They are responsible for guiding and supporting individuals in developing a deep understanding of themselves and their interactions with AI technologies.

Parents have the opportunity to create

an open and supportive environment where discussions about AI's impact on personal lives, privacy, and decision-making can take place. They can encourage critical thinking and help children and teenagers navigate the complexities of AI by fostering conversations that explore the ethical, social, and emotional implications of AI use. Parents can promote reflection, empathy, and responsible decision-making by actively engaging with their children's use of AI.

Educators, conversely, can integrate AI literacy and ethical considerations into their curricula. They can create learning experiences that encourage students to explore and question the role of AI in society, encouraging them to consider its benefits, potential risks, and impact on various aspects of life. Educators can foster discussions promoting self-reflection, encouraging students to critically evaluate their values, biases, and ethical responsibilities when interacting with AI systems. By empowering students to become informed and conscientious users of AI, educators can help them develop a sense of agency and navigate the AI era more responsibly.

Both parents and educators can be role models by demonstrating responsible and ethical AI usage. By exemplifying ethical decision-making, maintaining privacy, and being mindful of the potential biases in AI systems, they can instill these values in the younger generation. Moreover, parents and educators can advocate for policies and initiatives prioritizing ethical AI development, ensuring that AI technologies align with societal values and human well-being. In the context of the AI era, parents and educators have a unique chance to encourage self-awareness in people. By stimulating dialogues, introducing AI literacy into schooling, and serving as ethical role models, they may provide individuals with the knowledge and attitude they need to use AI technologies responsibly, make decisions compatible with their views, and have a more significant impact on society.

ETHICAL AI DEVELOPMENT AND IMPLEMENTATION

ADVOCATING FOR RESPONSIBLE AI DEVELOPMENT AND USAGE

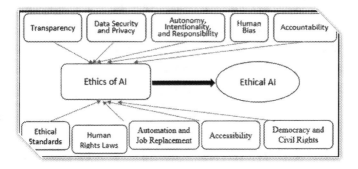

dvocating for responsible AI development and usage is crucial in ensuring that artificial intelligence technologies are designed, implemented, and utilized to benefit society as a whole while minimizing potential risks. Advocating for responsible AI development and usage entails actively promoting and encouraging ethical considerations in designing, implementing, and utilizing AI technologies. It emphasizes the need for fairness, transparency, accountability, and privacy as core principles in AI development. Responsible AI advocates strive to ensure that AI systems are designed to augment human capabilities rather than replace them entirely, fostering collaboration and enhancing human decision-making. Transparency and explainability are key as advocates push AI systems to provide clear explanations for their actions and decisions. Data privacy and security are emphasized to protect individuals' sensitive information and ensure responsible data handling. Advocates also stress the importance of accountability and governance frameworks, holding developers and organizations accountable for the impact and consequences of AI systems. Collaboration among stakeholders, including researchers, policymakers, industry experts, and the public, is encouraged to establish guidelines, standards, and best practices. Education and public awareness initiatives are promoted to increase understanding and encourage informed decision-making around AI technologies. Responsible AI advocates also support the development of adaptive regulatory frameworks that balance innovation with safeguards for responsible AI development and deployment. Continuous evaluation and improvement are emphasized to monitor AI systems, address risks, and mitigate unintended consequences. Advocating for responsible AI development and usage aims to ensure that AI technologies are developed and used in ways that benefit society while minimizing potential risks and negative impacts.

It also involves engaging with policymakers, industry leaders, academic institutions, and the general public to foster a collaborative approach to AI development and usage. By promoting ethical guidelines and best practices, we can harness the potential of AI while minimizing the negative impact and ensuring a more inclusive and beneficial future for society.

EXAMINING THE IMPORTANCE OF ETHICS IN AI ALGORITHMS AND DECISION-MAKING SYSTEMS

Ethics plays a pivotal role in AI algorithms and decision-making systems, shaping these technologies' impact on individuals and society. The ethical considerations embedded in AI algorithms are crucial for ensuring fairness, transparency, and accountability.

The pursuit of fairness is a critical part of ethics in AI algorithms. AI algorithms should attempt to produce impartial and equitable decisions that do not favor or discriminate against individuals based on gender, color, socioeconomic status, or other characteristics. Ethical AI algorithms aim to minimize the reinforcement of societal biases and provide equal opportunities to all individuals. Transparency and explainability are also essential ethical aspects of AI algorithms. AI systems must provide clear explanations for their decisions and actions. Transparent AI algorithms allow users and affected parties to understand the reasoning behind the system's outputs, ensuring accountability and enabling individuals to assess the system's fairness and accuracy. Ethical AI algorithms also foster trust between humans and AI systems by providing explanations, enhancing user acceptance and facilitating collaboration.

Furthermore, ethics in AI decision-making systems is critical in healthcare, finance, and criminal justice domains, where AI systems have a significant societal impact. Ethical decision-making systems prioritize the well-being, privacy, and dignity of individuals affected by their outcomes. They adhere to ethical principles, societal values, and legal requirements, ensuring that the decisions made by AI systems align with human rights and promote the common good. By incorporating ethics into AI algorithms and decision-making systems, we can mitigate potential harm and ensure that these technologies contribute positively to society. Ethical considerations are essential for maintaining human values, fairness, and accountability in the development and deployment of AI. Responsible and ethical AI algorithms and decision-making systems protect individuals' rights and promote trust, transparency, and responsible innovation. Ultimately, ethics in AI algorithms and decision-making systems are crucial for fostering a more just, inclusive, and beneficial AI-enabled future.

CALLING FOR COLLABORATIVE EFFORTS IN SHAPING AI ADVANCEMENTS FOR THE BENEFIT OF HUMANITY

Calling for collaborative efforts to shape AI breakthroughs for the good of humanity implies acknowledging that AI technology research and deployment should not be left to a single entity or interest group. Instead, it requires a collective effort involving researchers, policymakers, industry leaders, and the public to work together toward a common goal. Collaboration is essential because AI technologies have profound societal implications, ranging from economic and social impacts to ethical and legal considerations. Collaborative initiatives can ensure that AI breakthroughs align with societal values, needs, and ethical standards by bringing together various perspectives, information, and skills.

Such collaborations enable the identification of potential risks and challenges associated with AI and facilitate the development of comprehensive frameworks and guidelines. By involving various stakeholders, including those who may be directly affected by AI technologies, collaborative efforts can ensure that AI's benefits and potential risks are appropriately balanced.

Collaborative efforts promote transparency and accountability in AI advancements. Stakeholders can collectively shape policies and regulations that govern AI technologies by fostering open dialogues, sharing knowledge, and engaging in public debates. This collaborative approach helps address privacy, fairness, bias, and other ethical considerations, ensuring that AI is developed and used responsibly.

Furthermore, collaboration facilitates sharing of best practices, research findings, and resources, leading to more robust and effective AI systems. It also enables identifying and mitigating potential biases and unintended consequences, ultimately enhancing the societal benefits and minimizing potential harm associated with AI technologies.

CULTIVATING A HARMONIOUS COEXISTENCE WITH AI

ultivating a harmonious coexistence with AI involves establishing a balanced and mutually beneficial relationship between humans and artificial intelligence technologies. It requires recognizing the capabilities and limitations of AI while upholding human values, ethics, and well-being.

To cultivate harmonious coexistence, it is essential to prioritize human-centric design in AI systems. This means developing AI technologies that complement and augment human capabilities rather than replacing them entirely. By focusing on collaboration and synergy, humans and AI can work together to achieve better outcomes in various domains.

EMBRACING THE POTENTIAL FOR SYMBIOTIC RELATIONSHIPS BETWEEN HUMANS AND AI

Embracing the potential for symbiotic relationships between humans and AI involves recognizing that these entities can complement and enhance each other's abilities. Rather than perceiving AI as a threat or replacement, it is about harnessing its capabilities to augment human intelligence, productivity, and well-being. Symbiotic relationships between humans and AI can be fostered in various ways. AI can assist humans by automating mundane tasks, enabling them to focus on higher-level thinking, creativity, and problem-solving. AI can analyze enormous volumes of data and provide insights and recommendations, empowering humans with valuable information for decision-making. Moreover, embracing symbiotic relationships means viewing AI as a tool for amplifying human potential. Individuals can expand their knowledge, skills, and efficiency by leveraging AI technologies. With the help of AI, people may learn and develop at their speed thanks to individualized learning experiences, adaptive tutoring, and access to large informational databases.

In fields such as healthcare, AI can collaborate with medical professionals to improve diagnoses, treatment plans, and patient outcomes. Combining healthcare providers' expertise with AI's analytical power, symbiotic relationships can lead to more accurate diagnoses, tailored treatments, and enhanced healthcare delivery. It is important to emphasize that ethical considerations should govern symbiotic relationships between humans and AI. Fairness, transparency, privacy, and accountability must be integral to these relationships to ensure that AI benefits individuals and society while respecting fundamental rights and values.

Ultimately, embracing the potential for symbiotic relationships between humans and AI opens up possibilities for unprecedented progress and well-being. By combining human and AI talents, we can solve challenging problems, seize new opportunities, and build a world where human intelligence and AI technology complement and support one another.

STRIVING FOR A FUTURE WHERE SELF-AWARENESS THRIVES ALONGSIDE AI ADVANCEMENT

Striving for a future where self-awareness thrives alongside AI advancement involves recognizing the importance of human consciousness, introspection, and emotional intelligence as we develop and integrate AI technologies. In this vision, we acknowledge that while AI can possess incredible computational capabilities, it lacks the depth of human self-awareness, consciousness, and empathy. Therefore, we must ensure that AI development and usage are guided by the goal of enhancing and preserving these uniquely human qualities.

By prioritizing self-awareness alongside AI advancement, we emphasize the cultivation of introspection and understanding of one's thoughts, emotions, and values. This involves encouraging individuals to reflect on their interactions with AI, critically assessing the impact of AI on their lives, and maintaining a strong sense of personal identity and autonomy. In such a future, individuals actively engage with AI technologies while maintaining a conscious awareness of their own beliefs, biases, and ethical principles. They make informed decisions about AI usage, carefully considering its potential benefits and risks and proactively shaping the direction of AI development to align with their values.

Furthermore, fostering self-awareness alongside AI advancement means valuing emotional intelligence and empathy. Despite AI's ability to analyze vast amounts of data, understand patterns, and make predictions, it lacks the passionate understanding and empathetic connection humans possess. Therefore, prioritizing self-awareness involves recognizing the importance of human emotions, compassion, and empathy in shaping AI systems and ensuring their responsible and ethical use. By striving for a future where self-awareness thrives alongside AI advancement, we can harmonize AI technologies into our lives. This future emphasizes the development of AI systems that respect and support human values while empowering individuals to maintain their unique perspectives, emotional intelligence, and sense of self. We can fully utilize AI to improve our lives and build a more compassionate and inclusive society only through this convergence of human self-awareness and AI capabilities.

CONCLUSION: THE JOURNEY OF SELF-AWARENESS IN THE AI AGE

The journey of self-awareness in the AI age takes on new dimensions and challenges as we navigate the rapidly evolving landscape of artificial intelligence technologies. In this era, self-awareness becomes intertwined with our interactions with AI systems. As AI technologies become increasingly pervasive daily, we are prompted to reflect on our reliance on these systems and their impact on our thoughts, behaviors, and identities.

The journey begins with developing an understanding of the capabilities and limitations of AI. We explore how AI algorithms process data, make predictions, and influence our decision-making processes. This knowledge allows us to critically evaluate the information presented to us by AI systems and to question the underlying biases or assumptions they may carry. Self-awareness in the AI age also involves introspection regarding our interactions with AI. Whether it takes the shape of voice assistants, recommendation systems, or social media algorithms, we consider how AI affects our daily lives.

We contemplate how much we rely on AI for decision-making, information retrieval, or personal validation. Furthermore, it prompts us to consider the ethical implications of AI usage. We examine how our choices and actions affect others and the broader societal impact of AI systems. We evaluate the potential consequences of relying too heavily on AI or mindlessly accepting its outputs without critical examination.

Throughout this journey, we strive to maintain our individuality and autonomy in the face of AI advancements. We consciously balance AI's convenience and efficiency with preserving our unique perspectives, emotions, and values. We seek to ensure that AI technologies amplify our abilities and support our well-being rather than overshadow or erode our sense of self. Notably, the journey of self-awareness in the AI age also involves adapting and learning alongside AI technologies. As AI continues evolving, we must stay informed and reassess our relationship with these technologies. We engage in ongoing education and critical discourse to understand AI's latest developments, ethical considerations, and potential risks.

Ultimately, the journey of self-awareness in the AI age is a deeply personal and collective process. It calls for continuous introspection, critical thinking, and a conscious effort to shape the integration of AI into our lives in a way that aligns with our values, respects human dignity, and promotes a harmonious coexistence between humans and intelligent machines.

RECAP OF CRITICAL INSIGHTS AND LESSONS LEARNED IN THIS BOOK

Key insights and lessons learned in the importance of being self-aware in the age of AI include:

- Recognizing the capabilities and limitations of AI technologies.

- Reflecting on personal interactions and reliance on AI systems.
- Considering the ethical implications of AI usage.
- Balancing the convenience of AI with individual autonomy.
- Adapting and staying informed about AI advancements and risks.
- Aiming for the peaceful coexistence of humans and AI.

INSPIRING READERS TO EMBARK ON THEIR JOURNEYS OF SELF-AWARENESS

Embarking on a personal journey of self-awareness in the age of AI can be a transformative and empowering experience. It allows us to navigate the complexities of AI technologies with consciousness, intention, and a deeper understanding of ourselves. Here are some inspirations to encourage readers to embark on their journeys of self-awareness:

Embrace curiosity: Curiosity is the catalyst for growth and self-discovery. Be curious about AI, its applications, and its impact on society. Explore its potential while questioning its implications. Curiosity leads to knowledge, and knowledge is the foundation of self-awareness.

Cultivate introspection:

- Set aside time for reflection and self-reflection.
- Examine your thoughts, beliefs, and values and how they align with your interactions with AI.
- Consider how AI affects your decision-making, relationships, and well-being.

This reflective practice helps you understand your boundaries and the role you want AI to play.

Seek diverse perspectives: Engage in conversations and seek diverse perspectives on AI and its implications. Engaging with others who hold different viewpoints can challenge your assumptions and broaden your understanding. This exposure to varied perspectives fosters critical thinking and self-awareness.

Practice mindful engagement: Be aware of your interactions with AI. Notice how AI systems influence your emotions, biases, and behaviors. Develop an awareness of when and how you rely on AI for information, decision-making, or validation. Mindful engagement enables you to make conscious choices about your relationship with AI.

Continual learning: Stay informed about AI developments, ethical considerations, and societal impacts. Engage in ongoing education through reputable sources, discussions, and educational platforms. This continuous learning empowers you to adapt, make informed decisions, and contribute to shaping AI advancements responsibly.

Embrace human connection: Remember that self-awareness is not just about understanding yourself but also about understanding others. Cultivate meaningful relationships and engage in open dialogues with others about their experiences with AI. Connecting with others helps you gain insights into different perspectives and enriches your journey of self-awareness.

By embarking on your journey of self-awareness in the age of AI, you become an active participant in shaping the impact and direction of these technologies. Your self-awareness empowers you to navigate the opportunities and challenges of the AI era with intention, ethics, and a deeper understanding of your values and aspirations. Embrace the journey and discover the transformative power it holds for your personal growth and contribution to harmonious coexistence with AI and all of humanity.

EMPOWERING INDIVIDUALS TO SHAPE THEIR RELATIONSHIP WITH AI WHILE NURTURING THEIR SELF-AWARENESS

Empowering individuals to shape their relationship with AI while fostering their self-awareness involves providing them with the knowledge, tools, and support to navigate the complex landscape of AI technologies.

Individuals are encouraged to reflect on their values, beliefs, and priorities and consider how AI aligns with or challenges those aspects of their lives. This self-reflection helps you set boundaries, make conscious choices, and assert autonomy in your AI interactions. Moreover, providing resources and platforms for open dialogue and discussion allows individuals to exchange experiences, perspectives, and concerns related to AI. It creates an environment where individuals can learn from each other, challenge assumptions, and collectively shape the societal discourse surrounding AI.

Furthermore, empowering individuals to shape their relationship with AI involves promoting digital and data literacy. By equipping individuals with the skills to understand, interpret, and evaluate the information generated by AI systems, you can actively engage with AI outputs and make informed judgments. Ultimately, empowerment lies in providing individuals with agency and control over their interactions with AI. They should have access to tools that allow them to customize and personalize their AI experiences according to their preferences, values, and privacy concerns. They should also be able to voice their feedback, references, and suggestions to developers and policymakers, contributing to the responsible development and deployment of AI technologies.

By empowering individuals to shape their relationship with AI while nurturing their self-awareness, we foster a society where individuals are active participants in the AI age rather than passive recipients. It enables them to leverage the benefits of AI while maintaining a solid sense of self, ethics, and autonomy in their engagement with these transformative technologies.

It is essential to emphasize that artificial intelligence technologies. However, while they might help improve one's self-awareness, they are not intended to replace human connection, intuitive judgment, or the advice of an appropriately qualified professional.

Ethical considerations surrounding data privacy, algorithmic bias, and user consent should be addressed to ensure AI's responsible and beneficial use in personal and professional growth and **for all of humanity.**

Printed in the United States
by Baker & Taylor Publisher Services